Conquering Vocab:

The Most Effective Way to Learn GRE Vocabulary in the Shortest Amount of Time

Novall Khan · Michelle Greene · Shan Chen

Conquering Vocab: The Most Effective Way to Learn GRE Vocabulary in the Shortest Amount of Time

First Edition

....

A Little Life Lesson's Book

Copyright © 2009 by Novall Khan

Cover art copyright © 2009 by Novall Khan

ISBN-13: 978-0-578-02899-6

....

All rights reserved. No part of this publication may be reproduced in any form or by any means, electronic or mechanical (including photocopy, recording, or any information storage and retrieval system) without the prior written permission of the publisher.

....

To contact the author, write to: nkhan6@gmail.com

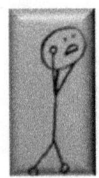

For Mimi

Table of Contents

Preface 5

Stories and Definitions 8

    Barbie and Ken's Aberrant Adventure on an Anomalous Island ... 8

    Jack's Audacious Retrieval of Water with Jill's Autonomous Help Along the Way 12

    A Lentivirus's Confounding Journey: Don't Be Craven, But Prepare to Be Daunted! 16

    Why Britney's Desultory State Led Her to Dissemble Shaving Her Head 20

    Distilling the Dogmatic 411 on the Clintons 23

    An Exigency that Calls for Exculpating the Silly Rabbit 27

    Max's Gullible, but Guileless, Heart 31

    The Indolent Actions of Bush Against the Inundating Condition of the Economy 35

    The Latent Teletubbies Reveal their Little-known Levity 39

    Goop, the Evil Genie: The Resulting Opprobrium of Your Ostentatious Wishes 43

    The Little Pandas' Quest for a Salubrious Habitat and Ultimate Satiation 47

    The Last Verbose Vocab Story: The Venerated Frat Party 52

Acknowledgments 57

References 58

So, what is the deal with this book, anyway?

This book was written by three students studying for the verbal section of the GRE, with the goal in mind to learn as many new vocabulary words as possible within the shortest period of time. Michelle, Max and I, began by writing a few sentences at a time, consistently incorporating words frequently found in verbal questions on the GRE. We would tack on a few sentences at a time, taking turns to pass the sentences off to the next person. Eventually, we had written a dozen short stories with absurd storylines, which to our avail taught us two hundred new words within three weeks.

At first this project was merely a quick and fun way to learn words, but soon realizing how effective our method was, we wondered why there weren't already GRE prep books like it out there. Having recently earned my B.S. degree in Brain and Cognitive Sciences, I began to see connections between this method of learning and the way in which memory and language are naturally processed in the brain. I conducted a comprehensive review of the cognitive studies demonstrating the most effective ways to learn, and sure enough, these guidelines matched the method incorporated into the stories we wrote!

So, where is the evidence that this method *is* the most effective method of learning vocab?

Simply put, the most effective way of learning vocabulary is by *attending* to it, by learning it in its appropriate *context,* and by deeply *encoding* it. Over the past four decades, research in the cognitive sciences has revealed that each of these components are involved in memory, and when utilized optimally, increases performance on such tasks as vocabulary comprehension.

Needless to say, this book was designed to maintain your **attention**. Each story is no longer than a few pages in length, and its absurdity and provoked familiarity of political figures, Hollywood icons, TV characters—you name it—contribute in maintaining your attention. When learning vocabulary, it is crucial to consciously attend to what you are reading. Mack & Rock (1998) demonstrated that people are only able to successfully recall what they have been attending to. Simply seeing a word on a page, for example, will not cause conscious recall. Furthermore, research by Glanzer & Cunitz (1966) demonstrated that when studying a list of terms, the middle terms tend to be neglected due to the lack of attention diverted to the middle, in comparison to the beginning and end of the list. This diverted attention causes the middle terms to be difficult to recall later. Thus, by keeping each story brief, attention is more equally distributed and every word will later be easy to remember.

The **context** of which vocabulary is learned is very important in contributing to the overall efficiency of what is learned. Studies have demonstrated that simply having a context when learning a word (rather than staring at a word adjacent to its definition) makes the word more easily recognized and later recalled (Rueckl & Oden, 1986; Spellman, Holyoak, & Morrison 2001; Jacoby, 1983). Additionally, reading about familiar icons increases the likelihood that the amygdala, the structure in the brain involved in emotion and evaluation of stimuli, will be activated. Buchanan & Adolphs (2004) demonstrated that the amygdala is involved in helping people remember emotional events, so simply by learning vocabulary in a familiar context should boost memory performance.

Perhaps most importantly, the level of **encoding** plays a key role in the efficiency of learning new vocabulary. Craik & Tulving (1975) demonstrated that when learning words on the most conceptual level involving sentence-processing, rather than involving categories or visual or auditory processing, for instance, words are more easily recognized during memory tasks. Thus, by providing you with deep encoding via sentence-processing of every word in this book, you will quickly be able to pick up on new vocabulary. Additionally, in the long-run, learning via sentence-processing enhances understanding, which ultimately leads to stronger and longer-lasting memories (Conway, Cohen, & Stanhope, 1992).

So, why aren't other vocab books just as effective as this one?

Many GRE books are designed to provide you with the vocabulary for rote memorization, but here lies the problem. Simply memorizing does not provide you with context, deep encoding, or even the maintenance of your attention. The automaticity of pairing a word with its meaning via flashcards, for example, takes a significantly longer time to develop than learning a word presented in a story. Furthermore, the automaticity gained by studying flashcards does not guarantee the understanding of the word on the level needed to answer questions on the verbal section of the GRE.

So, how exactly should I study this book?

Simple. Follow these 10 steps:

1. Read the first story all the way through, painting a mental picture of each event.

2. After reading the first story, briefly recap the main events.

3. Go back to the beginning and isolate the first sentence(s). Based on the context alone, make an educated guess as to the meaning of the bolded vocabulary word.

4. Check yourself. Look at the definition on the following page, even if you assume you already know the word. Many times there is an alternate definition to a familiar word.

5. Re-read the isolated sentence with your corrected understanding of the word, again painting a mental picture of it.

6. Repeat Steps 3 – 5 until the end of the first story.

7. A few hours later, return to the story to see how many definitions you can recall. Return to the story as many times as needed.

8. Avoid reading more than one story per day. It is best to focus on one section at a time to maximize efficiency.

9. Every so often, be sure to return to previous stories to refresh your memory.

10. Remember, do not simply flip to the definitions without reading the stories, and do not attempt to memorize parts of speech! Memorization is simply not necessary because definitions will come naturally through reading words in context.

1. <u>Barbie and Ken's Aberrant Adventure on an Anomalous Island</u>

Barbie and Ken were stranded on the "Lost" island. They began to look for plastic pieces from their bright-pink plane that crashed on the beach, but because the rain had not yet **abated**, their search was ineffective. Ken turned to Barbie and in his fake, semi-masculine voice observed, "The storm looks oddly **aberrant**; it must be a hurricane. Barbie girl, we should hold our plans to build a raft in **abeyance**." Barbie glared at Ken and cried, "If we don't get off this island, how will I get my daily Botox injections!?"

Barbie was too busy complaining to even notice that a horrifying smoke-like monster was nearing the beach. Ken alerted Barbie with his fake voice, "Quick! We need to **abscond** from that smoke monster!" They began looking for a pink, plastic shelter to hide in, but were out of luck.

Fortunately, the monster was on an **abstemious** diet and did not care to eat them. Of course Barbie was unaware of the monster's diet and **admonished** Ken to be quiet and remain still. The smoke monster began to creep forward, and a light-bulb went off in Ken's hallow head, "I can poison the monster by **adulterating** its food!" Barbie scoffed, "Well that would be us, Ken!"

Unexpectedly, Willy Wonka descended from the sky and admonished Barbie and Ken against poisoning the food. "The Wangdoodles have very little **aggregate** food left after I took the Oompa-Loompas away. Please don't do that." Ken listened to Wonka with **alacrity,** but Barbie was more hesitant.

Suddenly, Barbie screamed as an Oompa-Loompa approached her, showing its **amalgamated** body of millions of tiny bugs, like Oogie Boogie from "The Nightmare Before Christmas." Wonka was sympathetic and alleviated Barbie's feelings by telling the Oompa-Loompa to sit. Ken began to feel **ambivalent** about Wonka because he was angered and jealous that Wonka was comforting Barbie. Barbie noticed these feelings building up in Ken, so that night, she decided to **ameliorate** the situation and calm Ken down.

Barbie knew just the trick. Despite their **anachronous** nature, Barbie dusted off her 70's bellbottoms and platform shoes and held a little disco dance party. Ken's dancing was surely **analogous** to dancers on "Dancing with the Stars," and Barbie was impressed. Soon into the night, the party was broken up when Wonka received word via radio that his Oompa-Loompas were in a state of **anarchy** at the chocolate factory. He immediately called for his airship and asked Barbie and Ken to come with him.

As Barbie and Ken stepped aboard the airship, they noticed something a bit **anomalous** - all of the furniture had been dipped in chocolate and rolled in sprinkles. Wonka **apprised** Barbie and Ken not to eat the furniture, but it was too difficult for Barbie to resist (after all, she had been abstemious her entire life!). After Barbie took her first bite, she could not stop licking her lips in **approbation.**

Ken began ripping up the base of the airship, **appropriating** the most delicious part that he intended to save for dinner: the rudder. Suddenly, the airship began to plummet and within minutes, Barbie, Ken and Wonka were back on the "Lost" island in an unknown time period. Eventually, a few seasons later, ABC decided to save Barbie, Ken, and Wonka, but not before playing a practical joke on them by subjecting them to time travel.

Abate
to reduce in amount, intensity; to lessen

Aberrant
deviating from the normal or accepted way

Abeyance
temporary inactivity; suspension (e.g. holding a problem in abeyance)

Abscond
to depart suddenly and secretly, esp. to avoid capture

Abstemious
sparingly eating and drinking

Admonish
to advise against doing something

Adulterate
to make impure by adding cheaper or inferior materials

Aggregate
combined; total (e.g. the aggregate amount of experience)

Alacrity
willingness; promptness (e.g. accepting the job with alacrity)

Amalgamate
to unite; merge

Ambivalence
fluctuation or uncertainty, esp. when unable to make a choice or wanting to do two opposing things

Ameliorate
to improve or make better

Anachronism
something or someone not in the correct time period

Analogous
corresponding in some way, such as function (e.g. analogous organs)

Anarchy
a state of society lacking government

Anomalous
irregular; abnormal; unusual

Apprise
to inform; advise (e.g. to be apprised of your score on the GRE)

Approbation
commendation; approval

Appropriate
to take without permission; seize

2. <u>Jack's Audacious Retrieval of Water with Jill's Autonomous Help Along the Way</u>

When Jack and Jill began the **arduous** task of hauling their pail up the hill, they did not foresee who would be waiting for them at the top. At the top sat an **artless** troll who greeted them with a childish smile. This troll was also an **ascetic**, though seemingly frightening with its green wart-covered body, was wearing a robe and sat in a yoga pose. His focus was **assiduous,** such that he continued chanting and humming and snapping his fingers to the beat without regard to the presence of his new visitors.

Because Jack and Jill were heavily panting, the troll took notice and advised them, "To **assuage** your pain, use the force you must." Jack's knees began to **attenuate** as he realized that the troll was right; physical strength was not enough to make it up this hill. It would take a force much more **audacious** than mere walking in order to achieve their lifelong dream of filling that damn pail; they were going to have to use the power of the riverdance.

Suddenly, two **austere**-looking Irish boys skipped sternly up the hill past Jack and Jill. Together the Irish boys were an **autonomous** pair from the rest of those on the hill, but Jill didn't let that stop her from seeking their help. She whipped her long blond hair in the wind, imitating a Pantene Pro-V commercial, and successfully caught their attention. The boys stopped, and Jill asked in a sweet voice, "Can you teach me the secrets of the riverdance to help Jack and I fetch our pail of water?" The Irish boys **averred** that they were indeed the Lords of the Dance and that it would take thighs of steel in order to mount this anomalous mountain.

"Dance for me!" exclaimed one of the Irish boys. Jill attempted to dance while Jack looked at her blankly. "No, no! That's **banal**, weak, worthless!" shouted the other boy. Jill's poor riverdancing attempt **belied** her sudden ability to climb the mountain even quicker than the Irish boys! It seemed that Jill's desire to impress her austere instructors was **beneficent** towards her attempt to access the inner force the troll had spoken of.

Suddenly, a meteor lit up the sky, and it was headed straight for Jill! The little green troll grunted and **bolstered** the air in front of Jill with some sort of force field and the meteor was instantly destroyed upon impact.

The troll was **bombastic** after having saved Jill from the meteor, but despite his inflated attitude, Jack and Jill were very grateful. The Irish boys, on the other hand, **boorishly** played on Jill's vulnerability by snickering, "The troll must have saved you because he expected a little *somethin' somethin'*." Jill was so flustered that she yearned for vengeance. She twitched her nose like Samantha Stephens in "Bewitched," and ominously, three-leaf—rather than four-leaf—clovers **burgeoned** all over the Irish boys' chests. The boys then furiously counterattacked Jill by **burnishing** the bottom of her shoes, causing her to slip n' slide halfway back down the hill; making her that much further from filling up her pail.

Luckily, the quick-thinking troll saw Jill's unwanted journey down the hill and, by crossing his arms and blinking hard like a genie, he caused a padded, **buttress**-supported wall to appear and cushion her landing. The buttress, however, broke upon Jill's impact, creating a **cacophonous** sound, and Jill was now riding on the wall that was slipping down the hill.

The Irish boys then acted very **capriciously**: feeling quite terrible for burnishing Jill's shoes earlier, they now magically whipped up a 2009 Porsche Cayman to bring her back up the hill. Upon safely reaching the top, Jill slammed the car door shut and **castigated** the Irish boys for their thoughtless and cruel actions earlier, threatening to sing in its entirety the newest, most agonizing, pop hit, "I Kissed a Girl." Despite Jill's intentions, this **catalyzed** the boys' desire to sing anyway, and they began to sing an entirely new song: "I kissed a guy…"

Jack, almost completely out of the picture by now, made a **caustic** remark at Jill and reminded her not to stray away from their mission, pointing right at the well only a few yards away. Of course we can't finish this story without ending it properly, so as Jill drove towards the well in her Porsche, Jack tried to catch up with her and, as the verse goes, broke his crown and Jill came tumbling (in her Porsche, of course) after.

Arduous
requiring significant effort; laborious and difficult

Artless
free from deceit; free from restraint (e.g. an artless child)

Ascetic
someone who pursues contemplative ideals, and for religious reasons practices self-denial

Assiduous
constant in effort

Assuage
to relieve or ease (e.g. to assuage one's suffering)

Attenuate
to reduce or weaken the effect or intensity

Audacious
daring; bold

Austere
strict; uncompromising (e.g. an austere professor)

Autonomous
independent

Aver
to positively declare; assert or confidently affirm

Banal
commonplace; petty

Belie
to contradict; demonstrate to be false or incorrect

Beneficent
doing or causing good; kindness

Bolster
to reinforce or support

Bombastic
assuming dignity or importance; inflated

Boorish
without manner; crude; insensitive

Burgeon
to develop or grow quickly; flourish

Burnish
to polish by friction

Buttress
a support with outward thrusts

Cacophonous
harsh or discordant sounds

Capricious
erratic; whimsical

Castigation
to criticize or severely reprimand

Catalyst
something unaffected while causing activity between two persons or forces

Caustic
capable of destroying or burning living tissue

3. <u>A Lentivirus's Confounding Journey: Don't Be Craven, But Prepare to Be Daunted!</u>

"A Lentivirus found its way into a new body. Upon arrival, it met a **coagulate** of red blood cells and similar-looking white cells with long coda propelling them deeper into the body. Its RNA made a **cogent** argument to ignore these bodies and find its prey: white blood cells…"

Being of **commensurate** dorkiness as the authors of that really bad **compendium** on the history of the Lentivirus, Max hardly seemed to notice how non-**complaisant** his story was to the rest us. Undeterred by the bombastic nature of the story, Max refused to **comply** with Novall's suggestion to write about Family Guy and instead went with his urge to disseminate his vast knowledge about the intricacies of the human body. Max didn't even try to write on a **conciliatory** topic, knowing full well that Novall would not **condone** his ideas and would later tamper with the story anyway.

Soon into his writing, Max was **confounded** when a giant, 3-foot-tall Lentivirus scurried across his tiled floor! He glanced at his TV, of which flashed a breaking-news alert warning viewers that Lentiviruses were attacking Gotham. The **contention** caused by the military and Lentiviruses had already destroyed several buildings and residential areas. The news reporters were **contentious**—some thought that it was the apocalypse and reasoned that the public should submit to the Lentiviruses' authority, while still others thought the Lentiviruses should be nuked.

Max was **contrite** about writing the boring compendium for it had brought about this doomsday scenario. With Batman preoccupied with his movie theater debut, however, Max alone would have to save Gotham from this **conundrum**. The only way to solve this **convoluted** problem would be through extreme creativity and tact. It was no time for **cravenness**; Max needed to draw on the lessons learned from his previous viewing of the best piece of cinematography to ever play at the dollar theater (the "Superhero Movie," of course) and utilize the power of a pair of tights to **daunt** the evil Lentiviruses into submission.

With his superhero **decorum**, Max felt ready to face the giant Lentiviruses and quickly headed out to the streets of Gotham. With his superhero optics gear, he was able to detect one of the Lentivirus's location with ease, and dashed right towards it. Max pointed his Ghostbuster gear at the Lentivirus, and without even resisting, the Lentivirus surrendered in **deference** to Max. Max was quite surprised that the Lentivirus surrendered without a fight, and began to feel slightly sorry for it.

Max lowered his Ghostbuster weapon, but the Lentivirus, no longer intimidated by the weapon, destroyed all of Max's superhero gadgets simply by touching them, and scurried off into the night. Max didn't give up, though. He **delineated** the Lentivirus on a piece of paper and showed it to a stray Gotham dog. The dog took one look at it, and within minutes located the Lentivirus.

The Lentivirus seemed to gesture some sort of apology to Max, so he decided to keep the Lentivirus as a pet. He **denigrated** the Lentivirus to point out its bad behavior, and because of Max's great disciplinary skills, the Lentivirus became a loyal pet for years to come.

Coagulate
to thicken; solidify; curdle

Cogent
convincing; believable

Commensurate
equal duration or extent; proportionate

Compendium
a brief account of an extensive subject (e.g. a compendium of biology)

Complaisant
willing or inclined to please; compliant

Compliant
obeying or yielding, esp. in a submissive way

Conciliatory
to gain or attempt to gain someone's kindness or friendship

Condone
to disregard or overlook; forgive or excuse (e.g. condoning an illegal act)

Confound
to confuse, perplex or amaze; bewilder

Contention
an argument or struggle; strife

Contentious
tending to argue; quarrelsome

Contrite
remorseful

Conundrum
a puzzle; riddle

Convoluted
twisted; coiled

Craven
cowardly

Daunt
to overcome with fear; intimidate; dishearten

Decorum
proper behavior, speech, dress, etc.

Deference
respectfully yielding in judgment or opinion (e.g. showing deference to a parent)

Delineate
to draw or sketch in outline

Denigrate
to criticize in a derogatory manner; defame

4. Why Britney's Desultory State Led Her to Dissemble Shaving Her Head

The media **derided** Britney Spears when she shaved her head last year, but little did we know that there was an underlying significance to her aberrant actions. Last year her head was suddenly **desiccated,** not by dandruff, no, no, this was far worse. Britney's **desultory** behavior of brushing her hair obsessively throughout the day attracted mini gnomes to the fallen strands on her carpeting.

When she first saw the mini gnomes, she created a **deterrent** by setting rat-traps around her house. However, the gnomes saw the traps before they fell for them and were quickly angered by Britney. Their **diatribes** against her instigated her to remove the traps, and Britney became **diffident** and ashamed of her actions. The gnomes tried to reason with her, explaining the value of her hair in the gnome community, but Britney kept **digressing** from the subject.

Noticing her discomfort with the issue, the gnomes tried to make up for this tension by playing a **dirge** on their handmade windpipes. Britney was not impressed, however. The gnomes' windpipe melodies were no comparison to her Billboard single, "Hit Me Baby One More Time." So, the gnomes had to quickly come up with a way to **disabuse** Britney of her false impressions of their musical ability. They became **discerning** critics of her single by telling her that when she sang "when something wasn't right here...," she was **discordant**. Britney was shocked beyond belief and started to cry. The gnomes looked at each other and silently agreed to be more **disingenuous** toward her music so that she would not cry again.

The gnomes tried to be **disinterested** to more appropriately judge Britney's musicality, but Britney was fed up. She no longer wished to share her home with the gnomes, so she tried to **disjoint** herself from them. When that didn't work, she **disparaged** the entire gnome community by contacting her publicist and spreading caustic comments about gnomes to the public. However, the public had **disparate** ideas about the gnomes and actually empathized with the gnomes' situation.

With this, all of the gnomes cast out of Britney's home were given shelter in various homes across America. The gnomes had succeeded in **dissembling** their true identity, and thus, since early 2009, stocks for shampoo companies skyrocketed because they began marketing "moisturizing" shampoos.

Deride
to ridicule; mock

Desiccate
to completely dry up

Desultory
random, wavering, unsteady; erratic

Deterrent
to keep someone from doing something; military strength or an ability to defend a country

Diatribe
an attack; criticism

Diffidence
lacking confidence in one's own ability; shy

Digression
a section or speech that deviates from the subject

Dirge
a song expressing mourning in commemoration of the deceased

Disabuse
to rid of a false belief or error (e.g. disabusing an imaginative child)

Discerning
demonstrating outstanding judgment and understanding

Discordant
disagreeable; incongruous; dissonant; harsh

Disingenuous
not candid; insincere

Disinterested
unbiased for personal interest or advantage; impartial (e.g. a disinterested judge)

Disjointed
separation of connections or joints; lacking unity

Disparage
to depreciate; belittle

Disparate
distinct; dissimilar

Dissemble
to conceal the truth of, or provide a misleading appearance to

5. Distilling the Dogmatic 411 on the Clintons

When rumors of White House scandal broke out, Bill Clinton sought to **disseminate** the rumor by proclaiming, "I did not have sexual relations with Monica Lewinsky." However, the people of the United States did not buy his words and began the **dissolution** of the facts of what actually happened. At the time, Clinton's statement caused quite a **dissonance** with the American government, but to Clinton, there were more pressing concerns than his sexual activities.

Clinton's pants began **distending** not only from the obvious, but from his diffusing waist. Such a gain would hinder his aspirations to diverge from his career in politics to begin a new life as a Sports Illustrated swimsuit model by the end of his presidency. For one week, Clinton detoxed in order to **distill** from his body the key elements of his former body-building figure. When he was ready to present a more aesthetic front to the camera, Clinton sought Monica's help. Monica **divested** Clinton's clothing and took pictures of his figure, in order to submit a convincing career-change proposal to Congress.

A few members of Congress were **dogmatic** about the issue and laughed at Clinton, but the majority of Congress was **dormant** and ignored him. Clinton thought of another way to **dupe** Congress. Instead of submitting to the normal barrage of boring handshake-in-front-of-gold-gilded-chairs photo shoots, Clinton began convincing the media to follow him and other world leaders to a more eclectic array of backdrops. To highlight the evils of "global warming," Clinton and Queen Elizabeth **ebulliently** frolicked, scantily-clad and sweaty, along a beach. The shoot had great **efficacy** in not only documenting his visit with the Queen for the media, but also allowed Clinton to begin collecting action shots for his future modeling portfolio.

Hillary, standing on the sidelines this whole time, had the **effrontery** to ask Bill if she could be in his next photo shoot. Bill scoffed at her, but Hillary wasn't joking. Later that night, Hillary plotted a way to disrupt his next photo shoot to show Bill, and the world, that she was more than just the First Lady. Hillary began to compose an **elegy** with lyrics such as "If Monica can do it, so can I," which, of course **elicited** a severe response from both Bill and Monica the following day.

Worried that Hillary would attack her, Monica disguised herself by **embellishing** layers of makeup on her face, then, she absconded from the scene. Hillary did want to find Monica, so she **empirically** deduced where Monica was last seen by viewing several security tapes. When Hillary found Monica and cornered her, Monica cried, "I only wanted to **emulate** your life! You have it all! Damn you!" Hillary puffed with pride only **endemic** to spoiled daughters (i.e. Hilton's daughter).

This pride was **enervated** once the two were interrupted by a Secret Service officer's cell phone ringing to the tune of Tina Turner's "What's Love Got to Do with It." It turns out, due to an intense and deep-rooted jealously of the singer's 80's-fro, any mention of Ms. Turner's music **engenders** a feeling of irreparable disappointment in Hillary.

Seeing Hillary's vulnerability resulted in an enhancement of Monica's feelings towards the First Lady. Temporarily putting aside their past differences, Monica and Hillary began an **ephemeral**, though joyous, period of esoteric and awkward friendship that led the pair to engage in several spa dates complete with side-by-side massages and pedicures.

Disseminate
to disperse; scatter or spread

Dissolution
a dissolving or breaking up

Dissonance
lack of harmony; discordant

Distend
to expand; stretch; swell; spread

Distill
to extract the essence of as if by distillation; filter; abstract (e.g. distilling ideas into an outline)

Divest
to strip; deprive

Dogmatic
arrogantly asserting opinions; highly opinionated

Dormant
inactive; abeyance

Dupe
someone who is easily deceived or fooled

Ebullient
full of fervor, enthusiasm, joy, or excitement

Efficacy
capacity to produce an effect; effectiveness

Effrontery
shameless or disrespectful boldness

Elegy
a poem or song lamenting the deceased

Elicit
to draw out or bring forth (e.g. eliciting a reaction)

Embellish
to ornament; decorate

Empirical
derived from experience or an experiment

Emulate
to attempt to be equal or better at something than someone

Endemic
belonging, or confined to a particular area

Enervate
to weaken

Engender
to produce or cause something

Ephemeral
lasting for a brief period of time; short-lived

6. An Exigency that Calls for Exculpating the Silly Rabbit

Despite his best efforts to maintain **equanimity** while in pursuit of the deliciousness of Trix, the Silly Rabbit was constantly flustered that his favorite treat was only for kids. Each time he tried to obtain another bowl, he was forced to **equivocate** about his true identity. But, alas, as most children are **erudite** in the art of costume design (continually practicing by disguising themselves as princesses and cowboys), the poor rabbit would almost inevitably be discovered each time.

Unwilling to give up on his quest, the Silly Rabbit at last devised a plan so **esoteric** that only he and other dutiful members of SRFPT (Silly Rabbits for the Pursuit of Trix) could ever understand its convolutedness. Unfortunately, the Silly Rabbit got in over his head and died trying to get his Trix.

The kids delivered a **eulogy** for the rabbit during his funeral. They tried to provide **euphemisms** for all of the horrible things they had done to the rabbit: "we didn't prevent him from eating Trix because we thought it was funny; we were trying to protect him from having an allergic reaction because we thought he couldn't digest gluten products…" They never thought that in doing so, it **exacerbated** the rabbit's self-esteem to the point where he did extremely dangerous things to obtain the Trix cereal.

The kids did everything they could to **exculpate** themselves from this tragedy, but also recognized the **exigency** of spreading the message that the Silly Rabbit wasn't a bad guy after all. The kids **extrapolated** that the General Mills publicity team were the ones to blame. To honor the rabbit, the kids began to design a new product targeting General Mills, one that was not to be taken **facetiously**.

When word broke out of the kids' plan to enervate the company, former employee Pillsbury Doughboy decided to **facilitate** their efforts. The Pillsbury Doughboy contacted his manager and **fallaciously** introduced a new idea to incorporate Chucky dolls in the next line of Trix cereals. The **fatuous** manager was unaware that Chucky dolls happen to be creepy, so he foolishly agreed to mass-produce the dolls with a General Mills stamp on the Chucky foreheads. The manager had a bunch of **fawning** yes-men, so he did not notice that he made a grave error in judgment.

The manager's actions eventually led to the **felicitous** downfall of General Mills. With this sudden absence of power in the cereal portion of the economy, a man named Mark Zuckerberg (the creator of

Facebook) decided to **fervently** pursue dispensing a new cereal product named Facebowl. Unfortunately, due to the use of new unstable, eco-friendly, gluten-free, woodland-creature-loving packaging, all new boxes of Facebowl **flagged** and eventually tumbled off of shelves at the grocery store near you.

Fledgling shoppers saw the dropped and dilapidated boxes scattered on the floor and mistook them for a sign that the sky was falling. They began to **foment** rebellion against the scalawag corporate bosses of the major supermarket chains.

Such uproar **forestalled** the federal government's plan to discourage Americans of their **frugal** ways in order to stimulate the economy and at last solve the housing crisis. Sadly, such measures would prove **futile**, resulting in a cereal-centered exigency that haunted both rabbits and children alike for years and years to come.

Equanimity
maintaining composure under stress; staying calm

Equivocate
to mislead or lie

Erudite
knowledgeable; scholarly

Esoteric
understood or known by only a few people (e.g. esoteric references)

Eulogy
a speech or writing to honor a deceased person

Euphemism
an expression substituted for a more offensive or blunt expression

Exacerbate
to increase the severity or violence of; aggravate

Exculpate
to free from blame; prove right

Exigency
a situation needing prompt action or remedy; emergency

Extrapolation
to make an inference from something known

Facetious
not intended to be taken seriously or literally

Facilitate
to make easier

Fallacious
misleading; deceptive

Fatuous
foolish or silly

Fawning
to show affection or attempt to please

Felicitous
appropriate for the particular occasion

Fervor
warmth and sincerity of feeling; ardor; zeal (e.g. playing an instrument with fervor)

Flag [v.]
to let fall; grow weak

Fledgling
new at something; inexperienced

Foment
to provoke (e.g. to foment problems)

Forestall
to prevent something by a prior action (e.g. to forestall a poor grade by leaving adequate time to study)

Frugality
not wasteful; thrifty; sparing

Futile
unable to produce a result; useless; ineffective

7. <u>Max's Gullible, but Guileless, Heart</u>

When the RA on duty caught a resident leaving Sharpe-drawn notes on the walls of the third-floor hall, the resident did nothing but **gainsay** the accusation. The resident gave Michelle a **garrulous** explanation as to why she was holding the Sharpe, but Michelle started tapping her foot and yawned. Max happened to walk by during the resident's digression, and **goaded** Michelle to just leave the freshman alone. Max told Michelle, "Hey, the university already **gouges** on our housing anyway, so what difference does it make if this girl is drawing a picture of Edward Cullen on the wall?"

Speaking in such **grandiloquent** terms, Max's words wooed the lonely freshman into an excited obsession. Michelle and Novall scoffed and departed the hall, leaving Max alone with the girl. Suddenly, Max was not feeling nearly as **gregarious** as the adrenalized freshman and he turned to a shot of tequila in order to match the enthusiasm of his new friend.

Unfortunately, Max was unaware that his tequila had been adulterated—by the freshman!—and instilled with a new property, making the drinker excessively **guileless** and unable to tell a lie. The deceitful freshman seized this opportunity to talk with Max and asked him for his credit card information. Because of the adulterated tequila, he gave it out willingly, with his only thought being: "But she's sooo cute!"

Later when he told Michelle and Novall about it, they **harangued** him until he learned his lesson. So Max, now depressed, went to the lab and **homogenized** some tissue samples with homogenous lab co-workers who were also interested in homogenizing tissue samples for research.

As Max was keeping busy in the lab, he noticed that his Lentivirus pet had followed him there! He tried to admonish his co-workers that the lab may be contaminated because of his 3-foot-tall pet, but they assumed Max was just making **hyperbolic** statements and ignored him. Max castigated them, "How can you be so **iconoclastic**!? If there is a contamination of the lab, the rules have always been to stop, drop, and push the red 'Easy' button!" Because of the tone of Max's voice, they immediately obeyed, as if they were practicing **idolatry**; Max being one of the gods.

Unfortunately, their effort to reverse the Lentivirus's contamination was unsuccessful; it seemed as if the damage done was entirely

immutable, impairing the lab's efficiency. Despite all of these setbacks, Max was **impassive** about the situation and continued with his experiments. Shortly after, however, a new lab assistant who was very female and very cute walked in the lab. This seemed to **impede** Max's efficiency yet again. Max tried to ignore the cute rays being emitted from the lab assistant, but he failed being **impermeable** to the rays and instead soaked them up like a sponge. Max still tried to hold his ground and remain **imperturbable** through this high-adrenaline rush, but he was just not **impervious**, as his spongy-behavior already revealed.

The cute assistant noticed Max's awkward behavior, and, having the esoteric plan to secretly obliterate the lab, tried to soothe Max. She was getting frustrated, though, because Max was just too **implacable**.

The cute assistant was about to **implode** because her plan wasn't going the way she wanted it to, and **inadvertently** mumbled "how is it that the boorish resident drawing pictures of Edward Cullen didn't keep Max distracted long enough to stay away from this lab!? Now I will never be able to conquer the world…" Max immediately snapped out of it, realized that he had unfinished decontamination to take care of, and snapped at her "I guess your **inchoate** assets weren't good enough to distract me!" And once again, Max saved the day.

Gainsay
to deny

Garrulous
talking too much; rambling

Goad
to urge on; provoke

Gouge
to overcharge; swindle

Grandiloquent
speaking in a pompous manor

Gregarious
sociable

Guileless
sincere; straightforward

Harangue
a passionate speech, esp. to an audience

Homogeneous
made up of similar parts; similar

Hyperbole
intentional exaggeration for effect

Iconoclastic
attacking venerated traditions or ideas

Idolatry
the worship of idols for religious purposes

Immutable
unchangeable (e.g. a true friendship is immutable)

Impassive
without feeling; stoical; calm

Impede
to hold back; hinder

Impermeable
not allowing passage; impervious

Imperturbable
calm; placid.

Impervious
incapable of being damaged or penetrated

Implacable
unable to appease

Implode
to burst inward

Inadvertently
unintentionally; carelessly; accidental

Inchoate
recently begun; not fully formed; rudimentary (e.g. inchoate ideas)

8. The Indolent Actions of Bush Against the Inundating Condition of the Economy

In early 2008, there was an **incongruity** between the Borg Collective and Species 8472. Both species thought that the other was an **inconsequential**, inferior race, so they declared war. It was **indeterminate** as to which species would soon become extinct due to this new type of natural selection, but eventually it didn't matter.

The **indigence** of the poor U.S. economy spread to other countries, and eventually, to space. Bush was extremely **indolent** during this time, **inertly** sitting in front of his computer playing "Hot Dog Bush" on addictinggames.com while the economy plummeted. When the state of the economy began affecting the Borg and Species 8472, their ability to purchase more technologically-advanced weapons was severely impaired, leaving their war in abeyance. The Borg was extremely P.O.'d, so they sent a proposal via e-mail to Bush, knowing of his extreme **ingenuousness**. Bush believed the Borg to be a completely **innocuous**, friendly species, so he listened to what the Borg had to say.

Obviously, Bush's actions were **insensible** and as a result, he was captured and assimilated by the Borg. Bush now became Borg, complete with cybernetic implants and a green glow. He returned to the White House, and when questioned, he replied, "When Arnold Schwarzenegger was the terminator, no one questioned him." He **insinuated** that it was okay to dress up as a cyborg that looked very much like the Borg. Bush's Cabinet looked at him and decided to ignore his newest antics. "At least it's not another **insipid** day at the White House." This **insularity** about the severity of the situation left both the White House and the country extra vulnerable to infiltration by the Borg.

The Cabinet's **intractable**, nonchalant attitude was **intransigent** until the sounds of a melodic Borg dirge began to blare throughout the White House and **inundated** the Cabinet members' hearing. Meanwhile, Bill Clinton was walking through the White House and noticed the Cabinet members rolling in agony. "What's wrong?" he asked. They shouted at him, "Can't you hear that?!" Clinton scratched his head and replied, "Well yes, it sounds sort of like my saxophone playing when I was younger." Apparently, Clinton had been **inured** to harsh sounds; his childhood was filled with musical **invectives**. Perhaps that explains why Bush always felt **irascible** when he was invited to Clinton's house.

While the rest of the Cabinet held an **irresolute** plan of action due to the cacophonous sounds distracting them from the Borg, Clinton had a brilliant idea: to drive the Borg away by playing Clinton's competing elegies on all of the satellite radio stations! Clinton **laconically** explained his plan to the Cabinet, and although it was a regrettable decision, they knew what had to be done. Once the Borg accepted defeat—that Clinton's music was far more superior to theirs—they dolefully surrendered with **lassitude**. Maybe Clinton's inharmonious music could have influenced Bush's ability (or lack thereof) to solve the economy's problems as well!

Incongruity
not harmonious; inconsistent; inappropriate; absurdity

Inconsequential
unimportant; insignificant

Indeterminate
uncertain; indefinite

Indigence
poverty

Indolent
lazy

Inert
unable to move; inactive

Ingenuous
naive and trusting; unsophisticated

Innocuous
harmless

Insensible
unaware; unconscious; unresponsive (e.g. insensible to criticism)

Insinuate
to imply; hint

Insipid
lacking flavor; tasteless; dull

Insularity
narrow-mindedness; isolation (e.g. insular attitudes toward a political party)

Intractable
difficult to manage; stubborn; unyielding

Intransigence
refusal of any compromise; inflexible

Inundate
to overwhelm; submerge (e.g. inundated with homework)

Inured
to make accustomed to; hardened (e.g. inured to cold)

Invective [n.]
critical or abusive language

Irascible
easily angered; irritable

Irresolute
uncertain how to act; weak

Laconic
brief and to the point; concise

Lassitude
slow; sluggish; weariness

9. The Latent Teletubbies Reveal their Little-known Levity

The Teletubbies were quite **latent** from the media for years, but they had always been **lauded** by both toddlers and adults alike. Many were unsure of what caused their recent lack of presence on the BBC, but perhaps it was simply because of Tinky Winky, Laa-Laa, Dipsy and Po's **lethargic** work habits. It wasn't until the Teletubbies saved their town from flooding due to the collapse of the **levee**, that they had once again regained the spotlight, despite their obvious **levity**.

The Teletubbies were a **loquacious** bunch. If someone were to eavesdrop on them, they wouldn't find **lucid** conversation, but rather, a constant string of goo-goo-ga-gas dispersed throughout their speech. Even if they seemed idiotic, they were a **magnanimous** bunch, as evidenced by their co-founding of "The Derek Zoolander Center For Kids Who Can't Read Good and Wanna Learn to do Other Stuff Good Too." All seemed swell except for that darn Tinky Winky who began to **malinger** in order to avoid rising to the call of the sun-baby to make it to work on time. In order to appear legitimately ill, Tinky would twist and bend his **malleable** triangular antenna into assorted shapes and symbols including Venus and Mars.

Po, much like the Palin **maverick** of the group, found this new ill-appearance "...truly sick, yo" and began to break the bonds of platonic-ness and asked Tinky, or "T.W." as he now liked to be called, out for some drinks after work. In order to keep this secret bond special, Po and T.W. began the habit of being **mendacious** about what they really had been up to and why Po had been found divested of her metallic square tummy screen one morning when the sun-baby called. Laa-Laa and Dipsy were mortified, and soon developed qualities of a **misanthrope**, blaming Po's and Tinky's spiritual impurities on Muggle influence.

Harry Potter just had to intervene when he heard of the heightening tensions between the Teletubbies, but his attempt to **mitigate** the situation was unsuccessful. After all, Harry Potter was known for his own angry hormonal outbursts, so he was an unlikely candidate to **mollify** Laa-Laa and Dipsy's abhorring feelings. Nonetheless, Harry Potter suggested a nice, friendly game of Quidditch, Laa-Laa and Dipsy vs. Po and T.W., to solve their problems, but Laa-Laa and Dipsy were too **morose** to play. Dipsy cried, "It's just not fair that we worked so hard for fame, and now that we have it, the Muggles have pressured Po and T.W. into being **mundane** little #$@%@#!!"

Harry gasped at Dipsy's use of profanity. Dipsy, a **neophyte** at cursing, smiled, and said, "That's right, you $#@! Mother #$@$@ wand #@$%@! Hermoine #$ @%@# ing $#@%%!!" Jerry Springer stepped in and said, "Now now, gentlemen, let's be calm about this." The **obdurate** Dipsy seemed to enjoy this newfound freedom of speech and continued cursing.

Eventually, Jerry Springer just let the Teletubbies and Harry fight it out. Dipsy got a broken nose, bent antenna, and crushed pride after Harry cast lightning on him. This caused Dipsy to revert to his original, **obsequious** nature and he apologized to everyone, promising to accept Po and T.W. for who they are. And all was well on the BBC.

Latent
potential but undeveloped; dormant (e.g. a latent talent)

Laud
to praise

Lethargic
lack of energy; drowsy

Levee
a river embankment designed to prevent floods

Levity
a lack of seriousness; frivolity

Loquacious
talkative

Lucid
easily understood; clear; intelligible

Magnanimity
generosity

Malingerer
someone who pretends to be ill to escape a duty or responsibility

Malleable
capable of being pounded into a shape; impressionable

Maverick
someone who is politically independent; a rebel; nonconformist

Mendacious
habitually dishonest; lying

Misanthrope
someone who hates mankind

Mitigate
to make less severe; appease

Mollify
to soothe; make calm; mitigate

Morose
ill-humored; melancholy; gloomy

Mundane
worldly as opposed to spiritual; everyday; commonplace

Neophyte
a recent convert; a beginner; novice

Obdurate
stubborn; uncompromising; inflexible

Obsequious
submissive complaisance or deference; extremely attentive; fawning (e.g. an obsequious gesture)

10. Goop, the Evil Genie: The Resulting Opprobrium of Your Ostentatious Wishes

It was a dark and stormy night as you were **obviating** your superfluous plans to go hang out with your dorky friends. Once you decided to ditch them, your eyesight was **occluded** by an unknown gaseous presence. The foggy air was quite **onerous** because you were unable to see beyond two feet of your surroundings, but within seconds, a luminous, masked figure appeared in front of you.

"I am Goop, the evil Genie. You have released me from my shackles!" You shivered from the **opprobrious** nature of the evil genie. Goop continued, "**Oscillate** this rag on my lamp, and I will grant you exactly three wishes." The genie threw around a bunch of smoke and lighting effects in an **ostentatious** manner. You ignored your gut feeling and decided to take advantage of the situation, greedily oscillating Goop's lamp.

"My first wish," you thought. "I wish to be a **paragon** of GRE test-taking!" The genie looked at you and shook his head. "Done!" Goop exclaimed. You jumped up and down, realizing that this could be your ticket to Harvard. You ran to the local test center, and signed up to take the next-administered GRE.

While taking the exam, however, you realized that you had no control over your answers. You had very **partisan** approaches, answering questions based only on single definitions, and, on an extremely biased basis, argued on the writing section that Paris Hilton airs better TV commercials than Verizon Wireless. Although it may have been a veracious essay, overall it was too **pedantic** for the ETS graders to understand; they assumed any essay with "Paris Hilton" in it wasn't worth reading at all.

After receiving a mediocre score on the GRE, you realized that you never had a **penchant** for standardized testing anyway, and thought that you might as well use Goop to just admit you to Harvard automatically. "Sure thing!" After oscillating Goop's rag, you were admitted to Harvard... Harvard's janitorial staff.

After cursing at Goop for a lengthy amount of time, Goop said "Well, stop being selfish. You might as well have asked me to solve the world's **penury** and hunger." You shot back at Goop, "If I had asked you to do that, you would have made everyone spoiled-rich and obese! You are a **perfidious** genie, with **perfunctory** grants!"

Goop seemed to tear up a little, but you remained **phlegmatic**. Goop sniffled, "I practice **piety** with my masters, and I try my hardest. I can move on to the next person on my list, if you wish to no longer be my master." "Well, who might that be?" you asked. "Mr. Stephen Colbert," Goop replied as he was **placated** by the thought of being on Colbert's show. "Then I wish to be Colbert!" you exclaimed as you oscillated the rag on Goop's lamp.

Goop obeyed, making your features **plastic** in order to mold you into Colbert's form; Colbert, the city in Georgia, that is. Ah, well you should have known; the **platitude** of each wish fulfills the "evil" in Goop's job description.

Obviate
to prevent by taking appropriate measures (e.g. obviating the risk of a lawsuit)

Occlude
to shut; close

Onerous
burdensome (e.g. an onerous workload)

Opprobrium
infamy; dishonor; disgrace

Oscillate
to vibrate like a pendulum; waiver

Ostentatious
showy; trying to attract attention

Paragon
a model of excellence or perfection (e.g. a paragon of scholars)

Partisan
partial to a person or a political party; one-sided; prejudiced

Pedantic
showing off or trying to impress others with what one has learned

Penchant
a strong inclination; liking (e.g. a penchant for rock music)

Penury
severe poverty; scarcity

Perfidious
disloyal; treacherous

Perfunctory
lacking interest, enthusiasm or care; performed only as an everyday duty; superficial

Phlegmatic
not easily expressing excitement or emotion; apathetic; calm

Piety
reverence for God; dutiful respect; devoutness

Placate
to appease; pacify; conciliate

Plasticity
the ability to be molded

Platitude
a commonplace or dull statement; trite remark

11. The Little Pandas' Quest for a Salubrious Habitat and Ultimate Satiation

In the year 2250, a **pragmatic** panda found a blender abandoned by humans. The panda was tired of eating bamboo shoots all day so he utilized the blender to blend his bamboo, instead. After discovering just how appetizing the bamboo juice tasted, he decided to bring the blender home for his wife and kids to enjoy.

He gave a short speech on how to use it, including a cautionary **preamble**. In the preamble, he told them not to use it during the daytime when humans might hear it. He explained that evolutionarily, they were in a **precarious** position and almost extinct, and that their survival depended upon keeping their distance from humans.

The little pandas thought their father was acting too **precipitate**, so they raucously played with the blender when their father wasn't around. Their father suspected the little pandas to be using the blender carelessly anyway, so they had to **prevaricate** themselves out of their father's speculations. They blamed the noise on the few **pristine** Quaker humans who, although slightly more technologically-accepting than the Quakers a couple hundred years ago, nonetheless refused to eat their meals consolidated into pills, and used blenders for their food instead.

The little pandas clearly lacked **probity**, and after months of lying, decided to go behind their father's back and confront the humans once and for all. After all, it was the humans who were so **prodigal** with the environment, causing extreme global warming and near-extinction for the panda species, so why should they have to live in fear? It was time for the pandas to **proliferate** their message and join together as one panda force, fighting against the humans' harmful **propensity** to destroy the earth.

The little pandas held secret meetings where they began to build bamboo weapons and design strategic plans to **propitiate** the situation and to **proscribe** humans from ever threatening pandas again. After dozens of meetings, the pandas still felt they only had a **qualified** strategy. This was partly due to **quibbling** over the small details of their plans, ultimately causing difficulty in moving their quest out of its **quiescent**-state. Finally, one of the pandas named Obama stood up and said "This is enough. We need change. We are a united pandas, and we can do this together." The pandas nodded and cheered in agreeance, and marched out into the **rarefied**, polluted atmosphere.

They marched right up to the first human they saw, Kobe Bryant, and demanded to be treated with respect. Kobe was **recalcitrant**, saying that it was an absurd request. "After all," he said to panda Obama, "I'm Kobe Bryant. And you're just a panda." Panda Obama stepped forward and began reasoning with Kobe, while the other pandas pointed bamboo weapons at him. After much skilled persuasion, Kobe **recanted** his previous statement and agreed that the pandas should no longer live in **recluse** away from the rest of the world. Kobe warned the pandas, though, that they must find **recondite** ways to be able to convince the rest of the **refractory** population. Kobe was not trying to **relegate** the pandas, but they nonetheless **reproached** Kobe's advice.

The pandas marched on. They came across a drunken **reprobate** who had been **repudiated** by his parents. Panda Obama began his speech, but the reprobate was so intoxicated that he picked up two of the pandas and held them as if they were the stuffed animals he won from a carnival game. Obama was forced to **rescind** his speech and **resolved** to move on to the next person. Unfortunately, the next person was **reticent**, and the person after that, and the person after that… so the pandas were feeling unaccomplished and on the verge of giving up. Suddenly, they stumbled upon a **revered** old man named Gandhi.

Gandhi, a **sage** in his own right, asked the little pandas what they wished to accomplish by their audacious acts of civil disobedience. Panda Obama replied, "We would like to be treated with respect by humans. We want a **salubrious** environment to prevent extinction of our species, and we wish to achieve equality." Gandhi **sanctioned** their request and did something very unpredictable. Gandhi oscillated the rag off of a genie's lamp, and wished for the exact words of panda Obama's request to be granted.

The pandas were in disbelief that Gandhi had such powers, but they thanked him, and returned home. It was all over CNN and even Fox News: the pandas were finally accepted by humans, and the pandas were from then on completely **satiated** with their place in the world.

Pragmatic
practical

Preamble
an introductory statement

Precarious
risky; uncertain

Precipitate [adj.]
rash; premature; hasty

Prevaricate
to lie

Pristine
untouched; fresh; primitive

Probity [n.]
integrity and uprightness; honesty

Prodigal
reckless with money; wasteful

Proliferate
to grow or increase rapidly; multiply; spread

Propensity
a natural inclination or tendency (e.g. a propensity to gamble)

Propitiate
to appease; conciliate

Proscribe
to prohibit; ostracize; outlaw; banish

Qualified [adj.]
limited; restricted

Quibble
minor objection or complaint; petty criticism

Quiescent
at rest; dormant; still; temporarily inactive

Rarefied
made less dense (e.g. to rarefy a gas)

Recalcitrant
determined to resist authority; difficult to deal with; unruly

Recant
retract a statement; disclaim; disavow

Recluse
someone who lives in seclusion from society; hermit; loner

Recondite
difficult to understand; abstruse; profound

Refractory
difficult to manage; disobedient; stubborn

Relegate
to banish to an inferior position; assign; delegate

Reproach
to express disapproval or disappointment; find fault with

Reprobate
a sinful person; morally depraved; unprincipled

Repudiate
to reject with disapproval; disown; disavow

Rescind
to cancel; revoke

Resolve
determination to do something; firmness of purpose

Reticent
reserved; restrained; silence

Reverent
respectful; worshipful

Sage [n.]
a celebrated, wise person

Salubrious
promoting health; healthful

Sanction
to approve; allow

Satiate
to fully satisfy

12. The Last Verbose Vocab Story: The Venerated Frat Party

You **secreted** the Keystone Light bottle behind your back as campus security drove by. You were slightly **solicitous** about getting caught drinking on a dry campus, but you continued to walk towards the frat houses anyway. Because of the **soporific** day you had studying intensely for the GRE's, you were determined to have a little fun. This was a **specious** thought-process, however, because by the end of the night you would have experienced a whole new level of fun.

You took a few **sporadic** glances around to check out the potential for a good time, and clearly there was potential (i.e. the **stigma** of the frat quad was undoubtedly present). Despite your goal to only have a little bit of fun, you still didn't want to **stint** yourself at this party. Pimp-like, you walked over to the line of college students waiting for "admission" into the party. Everyone was **stolid**, regardless of your efforts to be noticed. The preppy guy wearing an ugly, **striated** polo, and even the drunk girl holding a **strut** to prevent herself from falling over, did not flinch when you took your place in line. You decided you needed a new tactic. Based on your observations of the social food-chain, you **substantiated** that you had to first make an impression with the ladies before you could make any impression at all.

You **superseded** your old self with the **supposition** that you could put on an act to win over the gorgeous girl standing a few feet ahead of you. You tapped her shoulder, and as she turned around you puffed your chest out and ran your fingers through your hair, with the hope that there would be a **tacit** agreement that you were obviously, the bomb. She looked at you in a **tangential** way, as if a guy like you could only ever have **tenuous** ties with a girl like her. Before she even said a word to you, you went on a **tirade** arguing that it was not fair how people judged you. "Look, I am just as worthy, if not better, of a guy than any of these frat guys here. Why not let me prove it to you?" And with that, she tersely replied, "Ok!" and she snuggled into your arm.

You began to fall into a comfortable **torpor** with her at your side, feeling her **tortuous** shape in your arms. Suddenly, though, she began to walk forward, **tractably** tugging you through the long line with her. She walked right into the frat house as surrounding guys' jaws dropped. You clearly committed a frat party's **transgression** by cutting the line, but at this point it didn't matter. You were in the party. People were dancing, jumping, drinking, playing beer pong, listening to "I Love College"—and you were in on it all. You began to play an intense, **truculent** game of beer pong, and won game after game, as your girl cheered you on. The more you began to win, the more you began to **vacillate**, stumbling over the beer pong table. It didn't matter though, because you were **venerated** as the new beer pong champion!

As the alcohol increasingly took effect, you became more **veracious**, truthfully spilling the knowledge you gained today through a **verbose** speech of GRE vocab words. Then it hit you: you had to get back to your room! You only had a day left before the GRE! It was difficult for you to navigate through the frat, as you were stepping on a very **viscous** floor, and on top of it all, your new "girlfriend" was making **vituperative** remarks telling you not to leave because she had plans to divest you of your clothing! You were in a **volatile** situation with the surrounding chaos of the party, and the **welter** of your brain beginning to revolt against you. You dashed out of the frat as soon as you could, ran back to your dorm room, and crashed on your futon.

The next morning, you awoke with a hangover, but you did your morning yoga and finished reading your GRE vocab prep. Reflecting on the previous night, you concluded that it was quite the **whimsical** experience, and you would have all the time in the world to live up to your new beer pong title as soon as the GRE was over.

The next day, you took your GRE's and without a doubt, aced it. And with that, you officially became a **zealot** of this book.

Secrete
to hide away or cache; conceal

Solicitous
anxious or concerned (e.g. solicitous about the economy)

Soporific
causing sleep; sleepiness

Specious
seemingly reasonable but lacking merit or incorrect; intentionally misleading; superficial

Sporadic
occurring irregularly; occasional

Stigma
a sign of disgrace or infamy

Stint [v.]
to be thrifty, set limits; frugal

Stolid
not easily stirred; unemotional

Striated
parallel bands; grooved; striped

Strut [n.]
a supporting rod or bar

Substantiate
to prove; support; verify

Supersede
to set aside or cause to be set aside; make obsolete; replace

Supposition
a hypothesis; assumption

Tacit
understood; unspoken; implied (e.g. a tacit agreement)

Tangential
only slightly touching or connected; digressing

Tenuous
slender; rare; slim (e.g. acquaintances held by a tenuous bond)

Tirade
a prolonged outburst or scolding; harangue

Torpor [n.]
sluggishness; lethargy; dormancy (e.g. an ill person's torpor)

Tortuous
full of curves or twists; bends

Tractable
easily managed; yielding

Transgression
a violation of a command or law; sin

Truculence [n.]
aggressiveness; fierce

Vacillate
to waver; fluctuate; indecisive

Venerate
to revere

Veracious
habitually honest; truthful

Verbose
wordy

Viscous
sticky; adhesive

Vituperative
verbal abuse; scolding

Volatile
evaporating rapidly; changeable; explosive

Welter
a state of commotion or upheaval; a confused mass

Whimsical
erratic; unpredictable

Zealot
a person who shows excessive zeal; passion for something

Acknowledgements

I would like to thank the contributing authors of this book, Max and Michelle, for all of their hard work and dedication for mastering GRE vocab with me. I would also like to thank the University of Rochester Library Staff for inspiring my love for books, as well as those who were involved in my Brain and Cognitive Sciences education at the University of Rochester. Without you, I could not have discovered the best way to learn.

Most importantly, to my family, who provided me with the tools for creativity, intelligence, and of course, a sense of humor.

With love,
Novall

References

Buchanan, T.W., & Adolphs, R. (2004). The neuroanatomy of Emotional memory in humans. In D. Reisberg & P. Hertel (Eds.), *Memory and emotion* (pp. 42-75). New York: Oxford University Press.

Conway, M., Cohen, G., & Stanhope, N. (1992). Why is it that University grades do not predict very long term retention? *Journal of Experimental Psychology: General, 121*, 382- 384.

Craik, F.I.M., & Tulving, E. (1975). Depth of processing and the Retention of words in episodic memory. *Journal of Experimental Psychology: General*, 104, 269-294.

Glanzer, M., & Cunitz, A.R. (1966). Two storage mechanisms in free recall. *Journal of Verbal Learning and Verbal Behavior*, 5, 351-360.

Jacoby, L.L. (1983). Remembering the data: Analyzing interactive processes in reading. *Journal of Verbal Learning and Verbal Behavior*, 22, 485-508.

Mack, A., & Rock, I. (1998). *Inattentional blindness*. Cambridge, MA: MIT Press.

Rueckl, J.G., & Oden, G.C. (1986). The integration of contextual and featural information during word identification. *Journal of Memory and Language,* 25, 445-460.

Spellman, B.A., Holyoak, K.J., & Morrison, R.G. (2001). Analogical Priming via semantic relations. *Memory and Cognition*, 29, 383-393.

www.ingramcontent.com/pod-product-compliance
Lightning Source LLC
Chambersburg PA
CBHW051717040426
42446CB00008B/930